CAVE ART

CAVE ART

POEMS

Charles Hughes

Milwaukee, Wisconsin

Copyright © 2014 by Charles Hughes
Published by Wiseblood Books
www.wisebloodbooks.com

Cover illustration and design: Dominic Heisdorf

Printed in the United States of America
Set in Arabic Typesetting

Library of Congress Cataloging-in-Publication Data
Hughes, Charles, 1951-
Cave Art/ Charles Hughes;
1. Hughes, Charles, 1951-
2. Poetry

ISBN-13: 978-0615924526
ISBN-10: 0615924522

For Bunny

without whom there would be no poems

Acknowledgments

Grateful acknowledgment is made to the editors of the following publications, in which poems in this collection first appeared:

America: "Ambition"

Angle: "The Cast," "Drowning and Seeing," "In Memory of William Sampson," "Look at the Birds of the Air," "Lullabies," "On Coyotes and Their Expanding Urban Presence Which Is Not Well Understood by Science," "On the Way to the V.A.," "Self-Help: Step One with Example," "To a Fellow Passenger of Ambiguous Occupation"

Anglican Theological Review: "The King Wore Two Shirts"

The Comstock Review: "Country Song"

Dappled Things: "Welcome Talk"

First Things: "Easter Spoils, 2012"

Innisfree Poetry Journal: "Dreaming on the Island of Burano"

Iron Horse Literary Review: "Christmas Pageant," "Lawyer Story: The Charity Benefit Dinner, 2005" (under the title "The Charity Benefit Dinner, 2005"), "Lawyer Story: The Settlement, 2001"(under the title "The Settlement, 2001")

IthacaLit: "Cave Art"

Measure: "The River's Gift," "Signs"

The Reach of Song, 2010 anthology: "Winter Song;" 2011 anthology: "Silent Prayers;" 2012 anthology: "Late Thirties Romance;" 2013 anthology: "A Day of Earth and Air" (recipient of the Edgar Bowers Award for 2013)

The Rotary Dial: "Darkness and Dave (Who Lived Down the Street When We Were Boys)," "Fall at a Park-Like Rest Stop," "January Evening, 10 P.M.," "The Lapedo Child," "November Song," "Spring"

Sewanee Theological Review: "Magnetism," "Poisoned," "Seeing Things Last Groundhog Day"

Verse Wisconsin: "Bumpy Air," "A Man at the Hospital, During Your Surgery and After," "Mornings After Thirty-Eight Years," "My Mother Looked at Photographs," "Night Vision, 1968"

CONTENTS

I. Bumpy Air

Welcome Talk...7

Bumpy Air..9

Ambition..11

The King Wore Two Shirts...12

Poisoned..14

A Man at the Hospital, During Your Surgery and After.........15

My Mother Looked at Photographs..........................17

Night Vision, 1968..19

In Memory of William Sampson...............................20

Darkness and Dave (Who Lived Down the Street When
  We Were Boys)..22

To a Fellow Passenger of Ambiguous Occupation...................24

Self-Help: Step One with Example............................25

The Lapedo Child...26

II. Story and Song

Dreaming on the Island of Burano............................31

Winter Song..32

The River's Gift...34

Drowning and Seeing...36

On the Way to the V.A...37

On Coyotes and Their Expanding Urban Presence Which
 Is Not Well Understood by Science...................................38
Late Thirties Romance..39
Country Song..41
Magnetism...42
Christmas Pageant..43
Silent Prayers..45
Lullabies...46
Lawyer Story: The Settlement, 2001..47
Lawyer Story: The Charity Benefit Dinner, 2005....................48

III. The Measure of the Year

January Evening, 10 P.M..51
Seeing Things Last Groundhog Day...52
Signs..53
A Day of Earth and Air..54
Easter Spoils, 2012..56
Spring..57
"Look at the Birds of the Air"...58
The Cast..60
Mornings After Thirty-Eight Years..61
Fall at a Park-Like Rest Stop...62
November Song...64
December Evening Walk...65
Cave Art..66

CAVE ART

I. Bumpy Air

WELCOME TALK
[Labor Day weekend, 1969]
for Dorothy Parkander

Saturday evening, after dark. Inside
Centennial Hall, a woman's speaking, reading
John Donne to brand new college freshmen. They're
Mostly tuned out, homesick, a little scared.
It is the delicate rhymes that catch their ears:
Away and *say; move/love; fears/spheres;* just sounds
Flirting with their attention, blending with
The dim interior and the cushioned chairs.
Soon they—five hundred plus—relax enough
To glimpse their sheer dumb luck they know can't last.
But trepidation of the spheres, / Though greater . . .
Images of the distant, bloody war,
In which they do not fight, spatter their minds,
Vivid as life. They know about real life
Already, what awaits them. Violence
Maybe. Impossible goodbyes for sure.
Our two souls therefore, which are one . . . Tomorrow,
A few of them will look up *valediction*
And try a studious hour learning the poem;
Someone will even write out the ninth stanza
For sending with a heartfelt letter. But

Welcome Talk

Nobody's thinking that far in advance
By now. *Thy soul, the fixed foot, makes no show . . .*
Nobody's thinking much at all. *Such wilt*
Thou be to me, who must, / . . . obliquely run . . .
The poem's parting sounds keep soaking in:
Rhyming, rising and falling cadences,
Live facts—*Thy firmness makes my circle just . . .*—
Becoming memory like other things
That happen and abide, happen and vanish
And still abide as part of who we are.

BUMPY AIR

Outside, the air's alive up here
(Six miles above the North Atlantic),
And none too pleased we're passing through.
The almost party atmosphere
Inside has vanished. Now a frantic,
More natural calm grips us like glue.

Dinner, its clink and chatter, cleared,
The boy's mom mouths, "He's two." His cry
Takes over, as a liturgy—
Which is by repetition seared
In the mind—can lift or mortify.
What words would come in vain to me

If you were mine to comfort? Drop
After deep drop, we hit some floor
And, shuddering, level off though not
For long. Then down . . . the next hard stop
Till . . . down. No children's ride. Still your
Plainsong laments our common lot.

Bumpy Air

"Big pockets full of bumpiness."
The captain's gloss. Be reconciled
To the uncertainties of flight,
He's saying. Sure. But if you're less
Experienced traveling in the wild—
A little Adam, the first cold night?

AMBITION

for Bunny

His, at the age of six, was to be Zorro.
Black hat and mask, a sword held in reserve—
He'd pull them from their closet pile, then swerve
Big figure eights around the houses, borrow
Whatever came to hand (they needed nerve
Those daylight raids), and take some puerile stabs
At self-disclosure—monogram, make Z's.
The mystery of stray baseball bats in threes
Puzzled clean lawns. Likewise, both up for grabs
Wet laundry and mere mud left scattered keys
To who he was inside. He doesn't try
These days; time's shorter now, and he's got less
And less to hide. His love's his best success:
She thinks there's more to him than meets the eye.

THE KING WORE TWO SHIRTS

Of all those facts, this one's the one I ponder.
What made me think of it this time was watching
A White Sox hitter spin away too slowly,
Get drilled in his right thigh by a hard slider,
And take his base as if he'd walked—not rubbing
The spot, not wincing, not changing expression
In any way that might be seen as weakness
(Per my TV, at least). *Stupid bravado?*
That's when King Charles loomed up. The First. Of England.

Our blind professor, way back when, could only
Rely on words tossed out to a dark classroom
Devoid of answering eyes. *Death meant a marriage.*
The day arrived, a January morning.
By evening, King and people would be severed
As head from body. So this King conceived it.
He'd stuck to his convictions, though defeated
In the long war, held prisoner, judged a tyrant,
A traitor, and a murderer. It was freezing—
Hence the two shirts. He didn't want to shiver,
To seem afraid to die. Stupid bravado?
He said he hoped to be espoused to Jesus.

The King Wore Two Shirts

A cough, not loud. Then off slipped the dark glasses,
Which tapped the air to introduce a coda.
You'll each do work of multiple kinds. The question
Haunts every task: whether it's done for glory
Or other gain or love. When it's that last kind,
You'll do it even if it comes to nothing.

POISONED

At night I think of that raccoon. He trotted
Along the sidewalk toward the house—toward us,
John and me, as we trimmed old shrubs grown clotted.
Strange: it was noon on a bright June day, plus
He ran too slowly, slightly side to side,
And maybe couldn't see, since we saw him
First, ten feet from where we stood. We both shied,
John and I, less afraid deep down than grim.
Rabies, John guessed; but later, poison struck
Me—why not?—though it could have been old age.
This would be such a little death to tuck
Away—so why consider causes? Rage,
Wants, wrongs, rights kill, not prompting much remark.
Still, those two black eyes stare out of the dark.

A MAN AT THE HOSPITAL, DURING YOUR SURGERY AND AFTER

I
"My wife?" No beard, but otherwise he looked
Like Lincoln. Tall, stooped shoulders, too long face.
Waiting like me, though he stayed on his feet.
He'd get no farther than the desk, then ask
His question. The woman, looking up, would smile:
"It shouldn't be much longer." She'd keep smiling,
Inviting him—"it's fresh"—to have some coffee
And sit down. "No, thanks." One time, his age came out
(Seventy-eight) and that this was his wife's
Third operation in three months. "A fighter,"
He announced. Most times, he just walked off I don't
Know where, and wasn't there to see your surgeon
Show up a little early, also smiling.

A Man at the Hospital, During Your Surgery and After

II

He sat, head bowed, a silhouette. Old Abe
Late in the war. The evening lights outside
Glistened—distant and cold as winter stars—
In the big window by his table, shaped,
And held him still. I moved, tray first, counting
On one last stroll around your floor—IV
And monitors all gone, your fingers pressed
Against my arm—and later talking turkey
With the nurse about the protocol for leaving.
His eyes, as I ducked past, stuck tight to his plate
Of pot roast, peas, and "home style" mashed potatoes
He hadn't touched. Praying for courage, maybe—
Afraid to eat and, then, have nothing left.

MY MOTHER LOOKED AT PHOTOGRAPHS

My mother looked at photographs.
That's how I knew Aunt Emma smiled
And Uncle Jim had been a child
Who'd take big chances just for laughs—

At ten, he posed, all nonchalance,
On the garage, umbrella raised
("To balance"—she'd remain unfazed—
"He's an accountant, it's what he wants");

How I found out life has its hells
Even for grandfathers—white hair,
Thin metal glasses, debonair
In paisley tie and wide lapels,

Mine dressed his up in "confident clothes"
(Which hadn't kept her from seeing through).
I'd search her eyes, as children do,
For signs of how deep down grief goes.

My Mother Looked at Photographs

This was especially true when she'd
Hit Edythe. Then her voice would fall
For emphasis: "We had a ball."
More friends than sisters, they'd agreed,

But all those times, she didn't cry.
She talked. She touched that teenage face.
A discipline, I guess. A grace.
Some deaths are hard to satisfy.

NIGHT VISION, 1968

That summer, back from Vietnam, Gene bossed
Our crew, part-timers still in high school. We'd
Wait in the seedy balcony—legs crossed,
Slouched deep in red plush seats—for him to end
The evening's show, turn up the lights to send
A blinking audience home, and then proceed
To point us to our putty knives and paint.
"How come you never talk?" Long afterward,
Told of his suicide, I glimpsed the ice
His eyes became, how differently the dice
Can roll. It wasn't—isn't—true: I've heard
Repeatedly his measured, soft complaint.
Last credits scrolled off-screen, the house again
Dark, bathed in night, he counts slowly to ten.

IN MEMORY OF WILLIAM SAMPSON
(died November 3, 1979)

I. 1969

He was just back from France, not fitting in.
The campus lawn lay waiting to begin,
All glints and blur in deep September heat.
He stood among the milling feet
(It didn't seem to matter where he was)
And talked as if he couldn't find
The words he wanted, words unkind
Enough for wrongs that death itself must cause.

II. 1970

The war, by May, had grown, turned uglier still.
Stage lights went up, making him visible
Before a crowded auditorium.
Words—like his own heart's blood—would come
And, in their John the Baptist fire, refine
My memories of that spring. What were
His odds? (Search "Greensboro Massacre";
There's video of him being killed online).

In Memory of William Sampson

    III. November 3, 1979

Death masquerades as everything. Night spreads
Its darkness, winter its snow. Even cool heads
Might not see through. Even soft hearts might harden,
Lose their capacity for pardon,
And come (his gun fired back, I've read) to grief.
If you had heard his soft heart speak
For peace, the peacemakers, the meek . . .
Well, horror dulls, but not the disbelief.

    IV. 2011

It is another spring. Wars multiply
On various fronts, gain self-esteem. Out my
Second-floor window, crows line up along
A wire, alert for rabbit young.
But now, two cardinals, streaks of scarlet, knife
Through blueness, sparking words of his
I can't help counting witnesses
To the implacability of life.

DARKNESS AND DAVE (WHO LIVED DOWN THE STREET WHEN WE WERE BOYS)

Her husband beat her now and then—
And, then, more frequently.
But once black eyes had multiplied
So no one didn't see,
She waited till a night when he'd drawn blood.
The cops did what they could.

They clubbed him a few times before
Dropping him in a cell.
He slept, practically comatose,
For days but woke to tell
The judge how he'd been hit at Anzio,
How friend turned sudden foe.

Too sick for jail, the judge decided,
And sentenced him instead
To the state mental hospital.
In three weeks, he was dead,
Leaving his wife an old white house and a son.
At twelve, Dave was the one

Darkness and Dave (Who Lived Down the Street When We Were Boys)

Who found him hanging by his belt.
I'd say that's probably why
Dave played these angry, solo games
Like *making gopher pie*—
Dave, decked out in his father's boots and hat,
Stomped gophers, mashing them flat.

It's probably why Dave fished a spot
Where woods and river met.
The water there held darkness and light,
Each perfectly offset.
He'd pull fish up into the shade, then dig
Their eyes out with a twig.

TO A FELLOW PASSENGER OF AMBIGUOUS OCCUPATION

You rode five blocks. You got on after me
By seconds. Sprinting past, I'd caught a glimpse
Of royal blue sweats bent deep inside a trash can.
Then, there you were again, boarding the bus,
Gathering scattered eyes, lifting head-high
A half-full plastic garbage bag—the bag
A whiter white than were your beard and hair.
"Dreams." You stood all five blocks, announcing,
      "Dreams . . ."

"The People of the Spirit claimed two souls
Per person. One gave life to body, one
(The freer one) to consciousness, to mind,
To the deep faculties distinct from body.
Nights, while the body slept, this latter soul
Wandered the spirit world and brought back dreams
To be put on like well-sewn, fitted garments,
To weave both souls together for the days."
—So, I imagine, you'd elaborate,
If asked. You could have been working that bus.
It's possible that you're doing the Lord's work.
You're maybe a prophet to an earthbound age—
Dressed down, unsober, homeless here and now,
Where souls break up and dreams get thrown away.

SELF-HELP: STEP ONE WITH EXAMPLE
for Rev. Bill Creed, S.J.

Night, and the day uncoils, unending.
When every avenue of thought
Loops like spaghetti, try pretending.

Say . . . you're a bird who's somehow caught
In someone's screened-in porch. You're still
A bird, however overwrought.

You rest five seconds on a sill,
Take off again, and bounce—some bird!—
To the floor. It's not for lack of will

You can't get out. It's the absurd
Escaping you that keeps you trapped—
The same as ever, only blurred.

The door's propped open now. Your rapt
Attention shunts: an enemy
(You think), his broom in hand, unflapped,

Attacks. You're at his mercy. He
Swings, misses, swings, and up you glide
Back to the trees, where you'll be free,

At home—yourself, but clarified.

THE LAPEDO CHILD
[Whose remains were discovered in 1998
in the Lapedo valley in central Portugal]

His bones are red. That drew me in among
The published facts and educated guesses:
Male, four years old at death; the burial some
Twenty-four thousand years ago and done
Carefully (*tenderly* might be more apt);
Head slightly raised, feet crossed, his left foot on
His right, a snail-shell pendant at his neck
(A nametag? Toy? Or maybe a holy vessel?);
And for a shroud an animal skin his people,
As if to register indelible grief,
Reddened with ochre, pigment that would bleed
And bleed all the long while the shroud decayed.

The find is interesting to scholars who
(Because his skeleton is early modern,
But with Neanderthal-like legs and jaw)
Say he's a puzzle piece, that he shows how
Much different lines combined to make the species
The well-stirred mixture we are now.

                                        I see

Him less as scientific evidence
And more as an every-child, a hybrid, yes,

The Lapedo Child

Touched by the double stain of love and sorrow,
Which travels like a family chin and—in
The inexplicable providence of God—
Spreads from each generation to the next.

II. Story and Song

DREAMING ON THE ISLAND OF BURANO

Burnt reds like radishes.
Icy, unearthly blues.
Tans, bright as a sand beach
In sunlight. Homes. To his
Mind's eye, the olives shone,
Shades of the trees. One peach,
Between two pinks, alone,
Lifted her out of her shoes.

Daydreaming, they forgot
Themselves, their distant, soon
To split up house, that ache
Now dully chronic. Not
For long, since love is cruel
(Their firm faith no dreams could shake)—
At best, a costume jewel
Set in a salt lagoon.

WINTER SONG

Winter blurred her edges as
Happens when the skies release
Burdens simulating peace
Over villages at night,
Each house, clasping all it has,
Soon anonymously white.

Cold announcing coming cold
Breezes under unlocked doors,
Finds old photographs in drawers
Stored like candles meant to be
Light for fumbling hands to hold
In a dark contingency,

Fades the pictures, fills both eyes,
So dividing other times
From this present season's mimes
Who, beneath their layers, long
For one face they recognize,
Well aware, like theirs, it's gone.

Winter Song

Dreams occasionally warm
Winter landscapes till they flow
Down familiar cheeks that show
Signs of what the winter does,
Also of another's form
As hers is and never was.

THE RIVER'S GIFT

Think back. Think back to when your eyes were stronger.
Remember seeing deeply into things?
Not magically, of course; unconsciously,
As children sometimes effortlessly do.
Being so young yourself, you'd come, back then,
To know—without a word from anyone—
The slowly flowing goodness in the river
Where summer days you knelt and fished, entirely
Riveted on the rod tip that at any
Second might jerk to life, and never doubted
The river's gift of those few weedy feet
Along its bank, a cast from feeding carp.
Arriving one mid-August afternoon,
You weren't prepared for this: dressed up grown-ups
Arranged around your small estate, all business,
Landing a sopping boy about your size.

Your obvious mistake embarrassed you
(You hadn't seen a drowning or a rescue),
Turned you away from visions that now seemed
Of little earthly use—the river's dark

The River's Gift

Benevolence, the unexpected boy
Whose face beneath his streaming hair was yours.
Suddenly lost in that familiar place
And drifting off some fifty yards or so,
Half-listening to songs of fading voices,
Their murmur of what could have been a prayer,
You stopped to try a futile cast or two,
Then started home, alone for all you knew.

DROWNING AND SEEING

How lovely now he's living without air.
The surface dims, the light disintegrates
In shards of rainbows breezes used to bear—
How lovely. Now he's living without air,
He seizes on these colors not for their
Refracted shades of meaning; now he waits.
How lovely—now. He's living without air.
The surface dims, the light disintegrates.

ON THE WAY TO THE V.A.

His face dips down in his fatigues. He smiles:
"This bus'll drop us almost at the door.
My wife, she's got her hands full of my files."
His face dips down in his fatigues. He smiles:
"She was gung ho, but we've put on some miles.
She says P.T.S.D.'s more goddam war."
His face dips down in his fatigues. He smiles:
"This bus'll drop us almost at the door."

ON COYOTES AND THEIR EXPANDING URBAN PRESENCE WHICH IS NOT WELL UNDERSTOOD BY SCIENCE

> "The coyote is out there . . . ."
> —*The New York Times* (September 27, 2010)

We humans have five senses and large brains,
But certain things we'll probably never know.
Some facts stay dark, although the fact remains:
We humans have five senses and large brains,
And kid ourselves that we hold nature's reins.
Then warning eyes one evening . . . So we grow.
We humans have five senses and large brains,
But certain things we'll probably never know.

LATE THIRTIES ROMANCE

If we had met in London then, the rain
Would not have kept us in. We are too young
In my besetting fantasy for rain
To matter much. We walk one afternoon,
Starting and stopping, talking—like this rain,
Unconscious of the moments ticking by.

"Hitler's insane," one of us cautions. "Time
Will tell," is all that can be said just now
(It's autumn, 1938). Now time—
Tearing hell bent, it seemed, toward war—has lost
Its way at Munich: peace. "Peace for our time"—
An echoed prayer we're half afraid to speak.

We say no more, content to watch the fall
Of cormorants from the invisible sky
To perches on the Serpentine, and fall
Ourselves through rain and time and not recover.
True, bombs have never fallen as they'll fall
In the next war. But public horror's vise-

Late Thirties Romance

Like grip's come loose—enough. We take a breath,
Walk past the anti-aircraft guns grown up
In place of plane trees. Not the slightest breath
Of gas masks or of plans for killing snakes
And dangerous animals in the zoo. Spring's breath
In autumn—bated, delicate. We know . . .

Much of this isn't real. Still, it's a dream
I'm glad to have. Something about it I
Find soothing—there's a reason people dream.
This one begins and ends in hopeless hope,
Which isn't the despair of a bad dream.
It's more—this dream—like romance or a prayer.

COUNTRY SONG

The transit system's broke. The buses run
Under Chicago rain like submarines,
Regardless—this bus east on Madison.
A woman in a Packers jacket sings
Some country song. She's blind, looks twenty-one
Almost, unlovely, short blond hair uncombed
By the downpour. Storms can likewise leave a tree
(And, if it's young, give pause to passersby)—
Dripping, leaves upside down, and patiently
Still, waiting for the sun. It's evening now,
The day submerged in its divisions. She
Sings on, sings what she sees right through the weather.
A lover cheats or dies, but the girl's OK
In the song—*floatin' over the verge of tears*.
We veer, slow hard. She stands, can't help but sway
Squeezing by others in the aisle, and falls
Silent, then disembarks the CTA
Into the weeping and expectant world.

MAGNETISM

Alone, adrift on incandescent seas,
Untutored in the poetry and prose
Of lightning flashing, bursting to expose
A future that would push him to his knees,
Uneasily he feels the current freeze,
Accelerate again, begin to close
The void between live poles, his own and those
His seek, then fuse inverse extremities.

Miles farther out, they've come apart—a he
And she—but float, still more or less in sync,
On ebbing, flowing waves whose chemistry
Can dull what pulls against this weakening link,
Lost in electric light (a kind of grace?),
Led by the water's intermittent pace.

CHRISTMAS PAGEANT

December twenty-fourth; already getting
Dark in the small spare room where she felt safe,
Though welts recalled the morning's dose of anger.
Her hand, about to switch the light on, paused—
Mother would come and not be pleased to find
She'd left the unmade salads (as she'd left
That stack of breakfast dishes for a rosebud),
With company and dinner in an hour.
Shadows would do just fine. She meant to practice
But, noticing the flower, dreamt a smile.

The sixth grade had their parts to speak at midnight.
Hers wasn't long; she knew it in her bones
Beginning now to warm beneath warm eyes
Awash, she saw, in pride and gratitude.
Her line got lost, the sun came out, and she—
Enveloped by a maze of wishful memories—
Stood at the trellis, picturing a vase

Christmas Pageant

Slender enough to hold the string-like stem
And not conceal her out-of-season gift
She didn't doubt would open with the day.
When fingernails bit into her shoulder,
The pain, for a split second, puzzled her,
And as she turned to face the angry present,
Her vision blurred, her part flashed through her head:
Let it be to me according to thy word.

SILENT PRAYERS

He'd clench both eyes at every siren's scream
Just long enough to speak his silent piece.
This oddball intercessory regime—
Triggered by fire truck, ambulance, police
Car or tornado—vexed and made her scold.
Stonewalled, she called a doctor (one last ditch
Attempt to figure out her twelve-year old).
The diagnosis: nonspecific twitch.

When he was over fifty, she too sick
For words, they met while there was time, her gray
Silences echoing the common prayer,
As two old friends might meet, let go of their
Misunderstanding, then at a certain tick,
Part company with nothing more to say.

LULLABIES

for Jim and Joan Leeney

He made a rocking chair for her,
She rocked and sang him lullabies.
They grew so old he wasn't sure
He made a rocking chair for her,
And sometimes, singing, she'd prefer
New words to light his dimming eyes:
"He made a rocking chair for her,
She rocked and sang him lullabies."

LAWYER STORY: THE SETTLEMENT, 2001

The call was set for two. He'd hung around,
Although the news from the East Coast got worse
And worse as that September day unwound.
"Settle," he recommended. "It's perverse:
Going to court—you're right, you'd probably win;
But you'd still lose, due to the legal fees."
His client's qualms that this meant giving in
Were met with math and practicalities.
About three-thirty, he put down the phone
And left an empty office for his train.
The empty city street proved echo-prone.
His steps came back, light tapping like light rain.
    Just as a mime can make things when he mimes,
    We fashion anchors in uncertain times.

LAWYER STORY: THE CHARITY BENEFIT DINNER, 2005

"Don't *Give* Up. *Build* Up." Buttons, signs, balloons
Aloft in Presidential Ballroom-A
All preached the legal clinic's can-do creed.
Dessert was chocolate mousse and macaroons,
A secular communion, you could say,
Embodying success, acquitting need.

His slim, half-full parfait glass he pushed out
Of easy reach. Speeches were coming next.
They'd instance how the clinic's muscles flexed
Against entrenched injustices and clout.
But now he heard a children's choir instead,
Small voices—"Standing in the need of prayer . . .
It's me, it's me, O Lord"—caught-up, true, spare.
Speeches did come. They seemed a little dead.

III. The Measure of the Year

JANUARY EVENING, 10 P.M.
[From our house]

An inch or so of snow last night. Tonight
The yard shines back cold moonlight at the moon,
And nothing moves—till a young Lab trots in,
Unbalancing the light and darkness. Shadows

Of crisscrossed branches fail in spots to stitch
Their fanciest embroidery on the snow.
Being a dog engrossed, you're not concerned;
Nor that your leash drags at your side, unmanned.

You stop. You stretch, twisting a resolute face
Hard right and up, as if to shed tight skin,
Pure animal certainty. Then off you go,
Down the back walk, then out, then down the alley.

Your life has ill-equipped you for the night.
Cars hurrying, wild creatures from the woods,
With sharper teeth and meaner streaks than yours,
Dead cold: they don't adore you. Then again,

Someone adores you and is looking for you.
He walks. He calls. He thinks (not angrily)
How similar to people dogs can be—
Needing their freedom, needing to be loved.

SEEING THINGS LAST GROUNDHOG DAY

Suddenly every April, like new suns
Born small, too small to shine for eons, two
Forsythias beside the house ignite:
Tight yellow swirls flaring up, the ones
That begin again. Then May comes, then they're through
With flowers, green, and out of mind and sight.

More snow sifts down. Bare, twining branches make
Matched hermit cells this morning. "Pray for me,"
She'd said—aware, afraid. But how agree
To the overflowing sky, another opaque
As twilight dawn, a little sister's pain?
Back to my shoveling. Time I learned to live
In the hushed, leafless earth, lie low, forgive—
For love—the winter, waiting fire and spring rain.

SIGNS

for an unknown child

A cloud can be a face in certain light,
Blotches of snow in March the candle wax
Left over from a party, dirty white
Beneath today's strong sun. I missed the facts
That night about miscarriages, their causes,
Frequency, odds irrelevant to me,
And took in stride your absence next to losses
That might have been--some other night, could be.
This just unveiled mud won't last. On wet,
Much older knees, I push the season hard,
Pressing these icy bare spots in our yard
With seed, counting the signs a decent bet:
A whiff of newborn warmth and its goodbye,
Changes becoming the dying winter sky.

A DAY OF EARTH AND AIR

Earth is so much a part of me
That, when I found a newborn bird
Dead on the sidewalk, death obscured
Spring's airier possibility.

It only took that faint reminder—
An ounce of skin, crouched, featherless,
Untragic in its naturalness—
To turn my heart more flintlike, blinder.

There seemed some shelter in that grave,
In the small surrender of hard soil
(Frozen till lately), in my recoil
From the depths that warming skies can have.

Dun oak leaves cartwheeled, came to rest.
As the wind's force fell, they'd fall—and then
Start kicking up their heels again
In gusts like breaking waves. Each crest

Set currents off: loose leaves at play;
Two cardinals sparking the noon glare;
Snowmelt, sun-colored, everywhere.
Things moved but didn't mark the day.

A Day of Earth and Air

Oblivious to the season's mood,
I spent a couple more hours raking—
While the earth plied its old undertaking
And the wind kept blowing where it would.

EASTER SPOILS, 2012

This is the end—for me, the beginning of life.
        —Dietrich Bonhoeffer
            (from his last recorded words)

Words to a prison friend, spoken in haste.
Gestapo men had come to transfer him,
Low Sunday, sixty-seven years ago
Today. The next morning, he'd be hanged with others.
No question who was strong and who was weak.
A room of prisoners praying, when the door
Burst open. *Dietrich Bonhoeffer.* He went
But only after saying his goodbyes,
Stealing a few more minutes as a man
Might steal his own possessions from a thief.
Words can survive the worst, which is love's trick;
Can, on occasion, be the love they praise.
On this distant Easter night, the world still writhes
In its uneven pain. Wakeful, I hear
Bonhoeffer voicing love's contingency,
Love's need, the thousand ways love dies and dies
And may live on in something someone says.

SPRING

A man and two small boys are digging worms,
Because it's Saturday. Clay soil turns up
In chunks—dark, heavy, holding day-old rain,
Baring sheer facets formed by shovel cuts
That glow like polished shoes in the May sun.
Sometimes it's hard to pull a worm out whole.
The worms don't like the light and desperately
(Especially the night crawlers) tunnel down—
Or try. There is an art: use too much force,
The worm will tear apart; too little, it
Will slip away. So when a wriggling gem
Makes its appearance on a mud-caked palm,
They smile, all three of them. So also when
The man digs the same soil another spring
(Dividing hostas by himself), he smiles
At worms he spots and at the broken earth
Still home to him, still soaked in slippery joy.

"LOOK AT THE BIRDS OF THE AIR"

Matthew 6:26

June. A late evening at the lake.
Our old—not friend exactly, though
We've known him close to twenty years—
Our host, I guess (he and his wife
Have run this place forever)—he
Stopped by our cottage by himself.
"She's up and doing now . . . No, no
More chemo. Wasn't going to help,
The doctor said." His eyes relaxed.
"We found the problem—low pH,
Too acid. Her new mantra is,
Eat alkaline . . . For counterbalance."

Out on the lake next day, the birds
Are solitary. Steadily,
A loon treads water in the middle,
Occasionally making dives, but always
Resuming, more or less, its post,
Keeping its green-black face to front
And silent as a sentry. There's
An eagle circling four tree-heights
Above tall pines fringing the point

"Look at the Birds of the Air"

I also like to fish, spread wings
So effortless you sense the strength
Of thermals lifting toward the sun;
A heron, too, gray-robed and still,
Vaguely angelic, standing back
In a small bay's declining shadows,
Knee-deep in lily pads.
                      I see them—
They float on water, wind and weeds,
Rapt in their element. They're not
Grasping at straws. On second thought,
Whatever else these birds may be,
Let me see harbingers of love's
Long lost composure, of a world
Where everything is bearable.

THE CAST

Arcing with gravity, the spinner bait's
A spark, yards off, of August sun. On one
Of many drifts across the point, two smallmouth—
Both swirling, diving desperation, stained
The lake's gold-bronze of cabbage weed-filled water
And early evening light; each, just a pound.
Always the memory starts this way: the flash
In the late summer sky, those startled fish
I gripped by their torn mouths before releasing.
Then turns to you. Curled up, book held askew,
You're dozing, safe in the rising dusk kept back
By the cottage's dim lamp's unblinking spell—
As if, from undimmed day, benignly cast.
So I imagined, coming inside with lines
Gone haywire, coiled like DNA, like love
And fear, tangles I never could undo.

MORNINGS AFTER THIRTY-EIGHT YEARS
for Bunny

Dear Amy, you begin, then glance my way,
Brow lowered, eyes raised, stage-waiting for attention.
You give the paper a shake. *My sister's boyfriend
Is coming to my wedding. He's in jail . . .*

Two squirrels out back chase up and down the ash.
Lighter late August air bespeaks the fall.
*He tends to be high maintenance. I don't want
To hurt my sister, but I also don't . . .*

It's our new breakfast ritual. You read—
Aloud—Dear Amy's daily correspondence:
Problems, pure trivia to life and death;
Each finds an answer (more or less), as if

Things could go on like this forever. We
Suspend our disbelief with Amy's help,
You reading almost earnestly, me turning
From breezy windows toward your voice. *Dear Bride . . .*

FALL AT A PARK-LIKE REST STOP

An hour by interstate west of La Crosse.
October leaves burn in the trees, burn out,
And drop—then gutter in their own dry streams,
In windblown rivulets that make us pause.
The early fall recalls the summer's drought
I've come close to forgetting. Now it seems

Stiffening leaves flow past our feet like clues
Of interest to an archaeologist
Or like a hemorrhage a doctor sees
Diagnostically as something he can use,
A road map leading to a ruptured cyst,
Let's say, itself perhaps spawned by disease,

A cancer. So inductive logic goes,
By reasoned steps, toward the incurable:
Pottery shards to settlements; from there
To a lost city, which in turn will pose
The further question why it fell at all—
War, famine, plague? Or climate change? That scare,

Fall at a Park-Like Rest Stop

The last—the sunlit leaves falling too soon
After a too hot summer couldn't rain—
Given the well-known wounds to earth and sky—
That scare is scaring me this afternoon.
It's therefore a relief when we again
Climb in the car, despite the silence. I

Can't help but be a little curious.
(Often what one has seen the other saw,
And thoughts—some thoughts—speak up unsaid.) I say
She's taking stock: there are the two of us;
We have two sons; we have two daughters-in-law;
We also have a grandchild on the way.

NOVEMBER SONG

Hostas die back, don't simply die. The first
Hard frost, I rake their raggedy leaves gone pale
And crooked, though the fall's been wet. You call me

To come indoors for lunch in your young voice—
A memory partly, partly a wish rehearsed
For years, for our long love. I'd sing you summer

And warm June rain, but we both know the yard's
Deciduous lei of limes, green-golds, blue-greens,
The roots now burning with a perennial thirst.

DECEMBER EVENING WALK

What's left of spring is gone in the first snow
Again this year. The schoolyard's all tucked in,
Dotted with starts of snowmen. Must have been
A little hard for kids, having to go,
Leaving behind short stabs at life instead
Of something more. Who doesn't know the feeling
(Not usually grownup grief, usually quick healing)
That comes from pushing or being pulled ahead?
A necessary lesson. That's my thought
As I move on myself, conscious of stray,
Soft flakes still decking out the like new air,
Unteaching, one by one, what winter's taught,
Brushing my face as kisses can—till they're
Borne frozen in time before they melt away.

CAVE ART

How often, only half-awake, I've lectured:
See beauty less as art and more as love;
And thought of caves (Lascaux, for instance), painted
In red and yellow ochres, blacks and browns
To make the horses, bison, ibexes

And stags, the aurochs, mammoths and cave lions
Long since extinct, which live on the cave walls,
Some charging, some in flight or in pursuit,
Others stampeding, butting heads or falling
(As one horse seems to—helpless, upside down).

Another chaos. I can recognize
That much from photographs. Inside the caves,
The painters left, in vain, what more they saw—
Stark, dazzling life that tugged them in and in
And still survives as art and evidence.

Cave Art

Some days, before it's light, I try imagining
The shadows cast by tiny sandstone lamps,
Feeling my way along a ledge with paints
And tools in tow, catching the warning sound
Of too quick footsteps not far off. You shift

A little, lace an arm around my shoulder,
Reminding me of morning and a love
Larger than earth's confusion—hidden, though,
Leaving to restless creatures room for visions
Of beauty they'd risk death for in the dark.

A NOTE ABOUT THE AUTHOR

Charles Hughes was born in Chicago, Illinois. He earned a B.A. from Augustana College, in Rock Island, Illinois, as well as a J.D. from Northwestern University, and worked as a lawyer for thirty-three years before his retirement. His poems have appeared in *America*, the *Anglican Theological Review*, *Dappled Things*, *First Things*, the *Iron Horse Literary Review*, *Measure*, *The Rotary Dial*, the *Sewanee Theological Review*, *Verse Wisconsin*, and elsewhere. He lives with his wife in the Chicago area.

Wiseblood Books fosters works of fiction and non-fiction, poetry and philosophy that find redemption in uncanny places and people; wrestle us from the tyranny of boredom; mock the pretensions of respectability; engage the hidden mysteries of the human heart, be they sources of either violence or courage; articulate faith and doubt in their incarnate complexity; dare an unflinching gaze at human beings as "political animals"; and suffer through this world's trials without forfeiting hope.

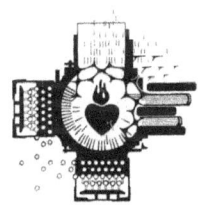 Wiseblood Books

Cave Art, by Charles Hughes is
Wiseblood Books' Inaugural Poetry Publication

Copyright © 2014 by Charles Hughes
Published by Wiseblood Books

Printed in the USA

Copyright © 2014 by Charles Hughes
Published by Wiseblood Books

Visit us at www.wisebloodbooks.com

www.ingramcontent.com/pod-product-compliance
Lightning Source LLC
Chambersburg PA
CBHW070206100426
42743CB00013B/3071